HOLIDAY POND

Books by
Edith M. Patch

NATURE STUDY

Dame Bug and Her Babies

Hexapod Stories

Bird Stories

First Lessons in Nature Study

Holiday Pond

Holiday Meadow

Holiday Hill

Holiday Shore

Mountain Neighbors

Desert Neighbors

Forest Neighbors

Prairie Neighbors

NATURE AND SCIENCE READERS

Hunting

Outdoor Visits

Surprises

Through Four Seasons

Science at Home

The Work of Scientists

HOLIDAY POND

by

Edith M. Patch

illustrated by

Wilfrid S. Bronson

YESTERDAY'S CLASSICS

ITHACA, NEW YORK

This edition, first published in 2020 by Yesterday's Classics, an imprint of Yesterday's Classics, LLC, is an unabridged republication of the text originally published by The MacMillan Company in 1929. For the complete listing of the books that are published by Yesterday's Classics, please visit www.yesterdaysclassics. com. Yesterday's Classics is the publishing arm of Gateway to the Classics which presents the complete text of hundreds of classic books for children at www. gatewaytotheclassics.com.

ISBN: 978-1-63334-050-3

Yesterday's Classics, LLC
PO Box 339
Ithaca, NY 14851

CONTENTS

CHAPTER I

AN INVITATION

SOMEWHERE, in a pleasant country place, there is a little lake. It is cheerfully called "Holiday Pond." The name itself sounds like an invitation to come and have a happy vacation.

Blueberry bushes grow on a hill near by; and the fruit, ripened in the sunshine, is very sweet. When you bend over to pick the berries, the sun makes the back of your neck feel warm at first, then hot. In spite of the juice in the berries you become thirsty.

So you go down to the water to bathe your face and drink and wade. After that you rest on the shore where some bushes make a cool shadow.

Then you forget that you have been hot and tired, for you begin to see the stories of Holiday Pond. Real stories—live stories—and so many of them going on at the same time that you may choose the ones that please you most!

There are frogs, those of each kind with manners of their own. The spotted pickerel frogs, sunning themselves in plain sight among the stones a rod or so up the bank, hop quietly to the water when you come near them. An old water-soaked trunk of a fallen tree makes a bridge across a corner of the pond. If you walk out on it the clamoring frogs that have been hiding there, plunge and splash into the water. They yell wildly as they leap and the first time you hear them you jump nearly as far as they do. They surprise you so! There is a calm bullfrog sitting on a broad lily leaf. His body is so nearly the color of the leaf that you might not notice him if it were not for his bright eyes. Those eyes watch you but the frog does not seem nervous. He does not bother to jump until you are almost near enough to touch him.

Some tiny painted turtles, all just the same size, are paddling about and stretching their necks while they hunt for their dinner.

Four young sandpipers walk along the edge of the water. Each bird calls to the others often enough to keep the members of the family from straying too far apart.

A damsel-fly, a dainty blue cousin of the dragon-fly, wraps her filmy wings about her body and creeps down the stem of a plant to the bottom of the pond. You can see her moving about in the clear water for many minutes, and you watch to see whether she will come up again and fly away.

The queer tracks at the margin of the pond are those of the raccoon who came down to wash his food before he ate it.

At the outlet, near the mouth of Holiday Stream are a lot of little fishes. They are ready to leave the pond and follow the stream to the sea. You would like to walk along the bank and go with them. But just then something flies down to the yellow pond lily and you creep as near as you can to see what it is.

So you stay at Holiday Pond and choose which of the real stories—live stories—you will watch. Perhaps some of them will be like those which are written in this book.

CHAPTER II

THE YELPING FROG

RANA, the green frog, stretched in his bed of mud and moss. He had slept without moving during the coldest days and nights of the year and now his long winter's nap was over.

The mud and moss had been frozen and he had lain in an icy nest, but the chill had not made him ache. He had known nothing about it. The colder his body was, the less it felt and when it was very, very cold indeed it became numb and felt nothing at all.

The sun of springtime warmed the earth. The blossoms on the willows grew big and furry. The ice was gone from the pond and the melted snow ran down the banks. Some of it flowed into Rana's bed and made a bath tub of it. The stiffness left his arms and legs and he kicked about in the water.

After a few splashes he found himself at the surface of the pond. He poked out his head and breathed deeply. It was good to draw in the warm spring air. He had hardly breathed at all while he slept the winter away, a stiff and numb little object.

Now that he was breathing and moving and feeling, he became hungry. A young water insect swam near and Rana swallowed it. It was soft and tender, and the taste of it pleased him. He had eaten nothing whatever for weeks and weeks and his appetite was keen. One small morsel was not enough so he hunted in the pond for the rest of his spring breakfast.

When Rana swam, his legs bent and then straightened out behind him. They were strong little legs and well formed. Even his toes were perfect in every joint. Yet a few years ago he had been a cripple for a time. He had an accident and one of his legs was broken off at the knee. He never knew where the lost part went. It disappeared very quickly. At the time there was a rather pleased turtle near by; but if the turtle knew anything about the missing leg, he did not tell.

However, the accident was not very serious, for it happened while Rana was a tadpole. A tadpole, as you may know, is fortunately able to grow a new leg in place of one he may chance to lose. Of course, since Rana had become a frog he would do well to be more careful of his legs. If he lost one now he would be a cripple for the rest of his life.

When Rana was a tadpole he had a small mouth and a tail that was longer than all the rest of his body. After he became a frog he had a wide mouth and no tail at all. Altogether his body changed very much while it was growing. It changed inside and outside. He even breathed in a different way.

A tadpole breathes with gills much as a fish does.

The yelping frog had a large flat ear on each side of his head.

The gills are on each side of the throat and are covered with skin. On the left side there is an opening or breathing pore in the skin. The water passes into the mouth and nostrils, flows through the gill chambers, and then goes out through the breathing pore. There is air enough in the water for the gills to use in breathing.

A grown frog takes in air through his nostrils and breathes by means of lungs. At least that is the way he breathes when his head is out of the water. He can breathe a little, however, through his skin—enough so that he can live at the bottom of the pond as long as he cares to stay there. A frog, happily, is in no danger of drowning.

Some tadpoles change into frogs their first summer, but Rana was rather slow in growing up and was a tadpole for two summers. The third summer he was a frog. That season he did a great deal of yelping. So did

6

all the other young green frogs in the pond. They sprang into the air and cried every time they were frightened.

Two boys, who were spending the summer at a farm not far away, often came to the pond. One day they ran pell-mell down the slope to the edge of the water where Rana and about forty of his kind were hidden among the sedges.

Suddenly, all about the boys, the frogs leaped into the air, yelled, and splashed into the water. The boys jumped, too. They slipped on some wet stones and fell into the pond with screams and splashes that were even louder than those the frogs made. Then the boys laughed, and after that day, whenever they met a green frog, they called him a "yelping frog." It was so good a nickname that other children who played by the pond used it too. So that is how it happens that a green frog in that neighborhood is known by the name which is used for the title of this story.

Even after Rana grew older, he still had the habit of jumping high into the air and falling to the water with a splash, if he chanced to be alarmed while he was sitting among the plants at the edge of the pond. But the cry he gave at such times was different, for his voice had changed and the old frog called a low and rather pleasant-sounding "chung" when he was frightened.

Early in the spring Rana had still another note. After he left his cold winter-bed he liked to sit in the shallow water near the edge of the pond and croak his spring song. It was a jerky sort of song, but it was the best he could do. There were neither words nor tune in his croaking, but there was joy in it. It seemed to mean that the frozen ground had grown mellow; the quiet, sleepy, stiff old earth was stirring and young again. Sap was running in the trees and bushes. Brooks were racing down their little valleys and chuckling as they went. The big butterflies with yellow edges on their brown wings, after dozing through the cold months in some hollow tree, were flying by day. It was spring!

So in the shallow water at the edge of the pond Rana sat and sang every night. He put so much force into his voice that his whole body jerked with every croak. The water was so cold that had you tried to wade in it, you would have shaken and shivered and stepped quickly to the shore. But it was not chilly to Rana. He was no warm-blooded creature who must wait until summer for his swimming. His little body, with cold blood inside and cold water outside, was comfortable enough. So he croaked and he jerked right cheerfully.

Rana was not singing a solo. He was singing in a chorus. All about him the voices of the other green frogs were croaking the same jerky, tuneless music. Another, different sort of croaking helped make the chorus louder. The spotted pickerel frogs also wakened early in the year, and they too sat in the water and sang at night.

It was during the season of the great spring chorus that Rana met his mate. Her throat was white and her ears were about the same size as her eyes. Rana's throat was yellow as an orange and his ears were larger than his eyes—much larger. Except for the color of their throats and the size of their ears, the two frogs looked very much alike.

Their flat, circular ears, at the sides of their heads, had no outer parts to fill with water when they swam. The eardrums were even with the surface of the head and covered with skin. Their heads and shoulders were bright, shiny green, and their backs were the color of olives. Their bodies were white underneath, and their sides were dappled with green and brown. Rana was nearly three inches long from the tip of his nose to the

Mrs. Bullfrog also lived in Holiday Pond.

end of his body (not measuring his legs), and his mate was nearly two inches longer.

Rana and Mrs. Rana looked, indeed, so much like small-sized bullfrogs that it would have been easy to mistake them for bullfrogs. Rana, however, had a little fold of skin along each side, reaching from his eye to the end of his body. So did Mrs. Rana. A bullfrog has no such side fold in his skin. If you ever wish to know whether you are looking at a bullfrog or a yelping frog, you can tell by the side fold, or the lack of it.

One day, rather early in the spring, Mrs. Rana swam off to lay her eggs. Rana went with her. An alder bush was growing at the edge of the pond, and one of its lower branches dipped down into the water. This branch seemed to please Mrs. Rana, and on it she fastened a clear, colorless, jelly-like mass. In the mass were her eggs.

It was a queer sort of nest, and after it was once in place Rana and Mrs. Rana both went off and left it. They never went back to look at it again. They did not know how many days it took the sun, shining on the jelly-mass near the top of the water, to hatch their eggs. When the young tadpoles began to swim about in the pond, Father and Mother Rana did not know their own children from their nephews and nieces. The old frogs did not feed the baby tads even so much as a single mosquito wriggler. The youngsters found their own food. Their legs grew on the outside of their bodies, and their arms grew on the inside, in the gill chambers. All this happened and the parent frogs paid no attention.

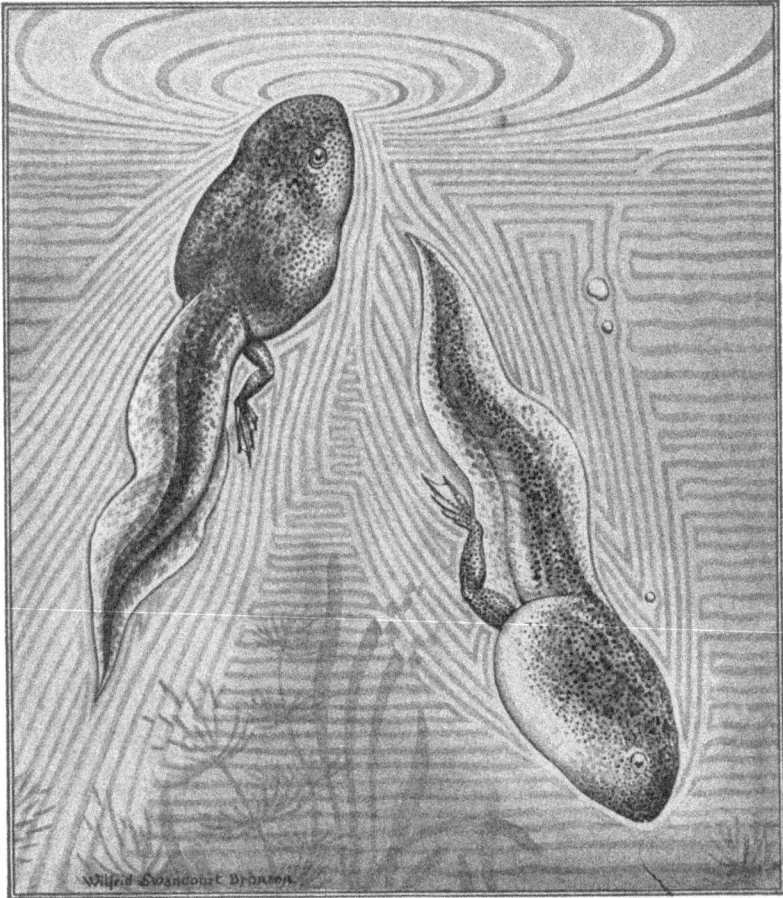

The young tadpoles took care of themselves.
They did not even know who Mother Rana was.

When they were old enough, each young frog thrust his left arm out through the breathing pore and went about with only one free arm. There was no breathing pore on the right side for the other arm to come through. For this reason each tadpole kept his right arm inside, and as it grew bigger and bigger it looked like a bunch in his side. When the arm grew big enough and strong enough, it tore the skin and poked out through the hole. So after a time each little tadpole had two arms outside instead of one arm out and one arm in.

It seems almost a pity that the parent frogs missed all the fun of watching their young grow up. If Mother Rana could have thought, "All our little sons and daughters are poking out their left arms to-day," it might have given her pleasure. If Father Rana could have croaked, "The youngsters have broken through with their strong right arms," he might have liked watching the growth of the tadpoles.

But it is the way of frogs to pay no attention at all to their young ones. And a very good way it is too—for frogs. With so large a family of tadpoles, it would be rather hard on the parents if they needed to take care of the little ones all the time their mouths were growing wider and their tails were growing smaller and their gills were growing useless and their lungs were growing useful.

Rana found enough to do to keep him contented. He hunted for his food. He did not take long hunting trips through the meadows as the spotted pickerel frogs did when they went out to catch grasshoppers.

*The spotted pickerel frog went into the meadow
to hunt for grasshoppers.*

Rana sometimes hid among the marsh marigolds at the edge of the pond, but he always stayed near enough to leap splashing into the pond if anything frightened him. In fact he spent about as much time in the water as the bullfrogs did.

Now and then, several times a year in fact, he molted his skin. His old skin would loosen on his body. Then it would tear down the middle when he shrugged his shoulders. After that he wriggled out of it as best as he could. He pulled with his legs as if trying to get his feet out of some stockings. He moved his arms as if taking off a pair of gloves. If he happened to be out of the water when he took his skin off, he usually stuffed it into his mouth and ate it. That was one way to get rid of it. If he molted under water, the old skin floated off out of reach and he did not swim after it and catch it.

13

There were plenty of kinds of food to hunt in the pond without bothering about his old torn skin.

On warm days he liked to sit on a lily pad with his head in the air. On days when the air was colder than the water, he was in the habit of lying flat on the bottom of the pond.

He did not lead a very busy life. Even in summer he had many idle hours.

As the days grew colder toward the end of the season, he was quiet most of the time. Then there came a day when the pleasant shallow edge of the pond no

One hot summer day three cricket frogs perched on green Rana's back, which was moist and cool.

14

longer satisfied him. His body had a queer feeling. He did not seem to like the light. The mud near by was black and soft. Slowly, very slowly, he pushed into the mud. Farther and farther he dug his way, until at last he made a little cave at the end of his journey. He felt drowsy—so very drowsy—and after that he felt nothing at all until the long winter was over. Then he stretched in his bed of mud and sought the light of a fair spring day.

CHAPTER III

LOTOR, THE WASHER

HOLIDAY STREAM ran through a muddy place soon after it left the pond. Near the edge of the water there were some marks in the soft earth. If a baby had been playing there and had pressed his fat hands into the mud, he would have made marks much like these by the stream. They could not be the marks of a baby, however, for they were not made in the daytime. They were left there at night when it was too dark for a child to find the way through the woods to the stream.

After the sun had set, one pleasant evening in May, Mother Lotor went for her usual walk. The shadbushes were white with bloom, and the plum trees scattered their fragrance through the dusk, but Mother Lotor did not seem to notice the flowers. She was hungry. She had eaten nothing since the night before.

When she reached the stream she paused a moment to look and listen and sniff. She did not rest on her toes like a cat or a dog. She stood with the bare soles of her feet flat on the ground, as a bear does. Because of the shape of her feet, the marks she made in the mud were somewhat like the prints of a baby's hands.

16

She was about thirty inches long from the tip of her nose to the tip of her bushy tail. The fur next her body was a dull brown, but the longer hairs were gray and those on the back were tipped with black. Her pointed head was shaped a little like that of a fox. Part of her face was whitish, but her cheeks near the eyes were black.

You have guessed by this time that Mother Lotor was a raccoon. It was so dark that you could not have seen how handsome a creature she was, if you had met

Mother Lotor was hungry.

her by the stream; but it was not too dark for her night eyes to see what was near her.

Mother Lotor was a skillful hunter and fisher. Her movements were both quiet and swift. She caught a few frogs and killed them so quickly that they had no time to suffer. She caught some little fishes and tossed them on the shore.

The frogs and fishes were quite clean. They had just been taken from the water where they had soaked all their lives. But Mother Lotor washed each one before she ate it. She washed it with her hands and she washed it with her feet. She squeezed it and she crushed it. She was in no haste. Leisurely she rested her back against a tree and held her food between her feet while she stripped the white meat into shreds and ate it daintily from her hands.

After her evening meal she went for a walk. She did not wander far, however, for five reasons. Each reason was a little Lotor, and each little Lotor was hungry. So she soon went home to feed her babies. She did not take fishes and frogs to them. They were too young, indeed, for any food except warm milk, the natural first food of all young mammals.

When they had sucked their milk they cuddled together and went to sleep. At first they had been blind and very helpless, but now they were old enough to open their eyes and to play with one another a little. There was not room for very much frolic, though, for their nursery was only a hollow in an old tree.

A woodpecker started the hollow years before, rather high up in the tree, near where a branch had been broken off in a windstorm. The woodpecker nested there one season, and after that some squirrels used it for a bedroom and pantry.

A tree frog found the rotting wood at the bottom of the hollow one cold autumn night when he felt the need to dig into some such soft sheltered place, so he spent the winter there. He liked his home so much that he lived there for four or five years except for a while each spring when he went to the pond to join the spring chorus there. After that season of song he found his way back to his tree hole and stayed inside on very bright sunny days. When the skies were dark with night or clouds, he came out and hunted and sang. His music was a pleasant trilly sort of purr.

As the opening through the bark became older and bigger, more and more rain and snow drifted in each year and the wet wood rotted. Big ants tunneled through the edges, and boring beetles made their trails.

So the woodpecker and the squirrels and the tree frog and the ants and the beetles and doubtless many other creatures had been the strange carpenters that had helped make the tree cabin large enough for the Lotor family.

The five little Lotors knew nothing about the other cave dwellers that had lived in their home before they were born. They knew nothing about all the strange world outside their hollow.

They did not even know their own father very well yet. He came and looked at them and sometimes he brought meat to Mother Lotor. She took such food to the pond or the stream and washed it. Perhaps Father Lotor had squeezed and pounded it in the stream before he gave it to her, but that was no help to her. She felt a need to wash it for herself.

For several months Father Lotor did much of his fishing and hunting alone, although he often met Mother Lotor.

One night early in July he went to watch a turtle nearly buried in the mud. Her head and the front edge of her shell were up out of the mud, but not much else showed. She had been there for almost a week and had not tried to get out. She had, indeed, buried herself in the soft ground and seemed in no hurry to move. Father Lotor had seen her a night or two before and had watched her then for a few hours. He had not disturbed her. She was a big snapping turtle, and he was not foolish enough to try to catch her even if she was deep in the mud. This happened to be the end of her stay, however, and at last she wallowed out and walked off with awkward thumping, dragging steps toward a pond that was half a mile or more away.

Before the old snapping turtle was well out of sight, Father Lotor was busy digging in the mud in the very place she had just left. He uncovered about three dozen eggs in their muddy nest, and the sight of them made him feel very hungry. He was not, however, a selfish raccoon, and he knew that Mother Lotor liked turtle

*For several months Father Lotor did most
of his hunting alone.*

eggs. So he called. His voice trembled, and perhaps
if you had heard him you would have thought the
quavering sound was the note of an owl. Many people
make that mistake. But Mother Lotor, who happened
to be hunting not far away, had no doubt. She knew
who spoke. A few minutes later the two raccoons were
seated beside the turtle's nest ready for a feast. In the
hands of each was a little ball-shaped egg. Each nipped
a hole in the whitish shell and drank daintily, spilling
hardly a drop. Egg after egg was eaten in this way until
the meal was finished.

Then Mother Lotor ran back to her five hungry baby raccoons, and Father Lotor climbed a tall pine tree and went to sleep in an empty crow's nest. One-third of his length was fluffy tail, and by curving his body until the tip of his nose was covered with the tip of his tail, he fitted the crow's nest very well.

Now and then Father Lotor would see Mother Lotor at the edge of the water when they happened to go to the same place to wash their food. One evening when they were together, they heard a cry. Perhaps if you had heard the sound, you would have thought it was made by a frightened human baby. But Mother Lotor made no mistake. She rushed to the hollow tree as fast as she could go. There, at the foot of the tree, was a little raccoon. He had climbed out of the hollow and slipped and fallen. He did not know where his mother was. The world seemed very big. The ground felt queer. He was so frightened that he whimpered.

Mother Lotor urged him back up the tree by following him and poking him with her nose. When he reached the hollow, she gave him a gentle shove and he cuddled against the other little raccoons, still whimpering with fright.

The next night Mother Lotor climbed to a branch below the hollow and called her young ones. Three of them went to her and liked the excitement of feeling the breeze against their fur and looking out in all directions into the night. Later the other two came out, and before many nights went by they would go down and up. They liked to play outside, and went into the hollow only to sleep during the day.

Perhaps Father Lotor knew what was happening at the home tree, for one evening about that time he went to the pond and called to his family. When Mother Lotor heard his quavering voice, she led the five little Lotors to the pond. There stood Father Lotor, and near him was the picnic dinner he had brought them.

It was a hen. The old raccoon had found it on a low branch of a tree near the henyard at Holiday Farm. The other hens always went into the henhouse to spend the night on the perches there, but this hen had the habit of staying outside and sleeping on a branch. The raccoon was strong and skillful, and he twisted her neck as quickly as a man could have done if he had wanted it for a chicken soup.

Father Lotor pulled out the feathers too, about as well as a man could have done that. Next he washed the hen in the pond. He squeezed it with his hands and he pounded it with his feet. Mother Lotor washed it too, just as he had done. Then she tore off some shreds of the meat and gave them to the five little Lotors. They liked their picnic dinner as well as you like chicken sandwiches. They did something to their morsels that you would not do with sandwiches. They washed them at the edge of the pond before they ate them.

That was the first time that the little Lotors ever went to a picnic with their father and mother. But it was not the last time. Indeed, every night now the family of seven hunted together or near enough to call to one another.

The fourth night out was an unhappy one for

Cubby Lotor. The evening started very pleasantly with a blueberry picnic on the hill where all the Lotors went together. It was the first time Cubby had tasted berries, and he ate the sweet ripe fruit busily until he found a rather large insect that jumped by means of long hind legs. Then he wandered off on a grasshopper hunt.

After a time he went down to Holiday Stream and played along the bank until he came to an old log that made a bridge across the brook. Cubby did not really need a bridge. He liked to wade in the water and could already swim very well. But all raccoons like old logs, so it was natural for Cubby to creep along this one. There, in the air, just over the middle of the log, dangled a bit of bright tin that glistened in the moonlight. All raccoons like to play with little shiny things, so naturally Cubby reached out one hand to tap the bit of tin. Just then the hard jaws of a cruel trap snapped and caught three of Cubby's fingers in a grip of pain. He was frightened and hurt, and he cried pitifully as he tried to pull himself free.

His wail of terror reached his mother's ear and she ran—oh, how she ran! She felt his poor hand quivering in the trap, and she did very quickly the only thing she could to save him. Her sharp teeth made three swift cuts and Cubby was free, all but the ends of the three fingers which the trap still held.

The next day the farmer from Holiday Farm happened to pass near the log by the stream. He saw the trap and a frown came in his face. When he noticed what was in the trap his frown grew deeper. He took the trap to the pond and threw it into the deepest water. Then he made a sign—NO STEEL TRAPS ALLOWED HERE—and nailed it to a tree near the log.

"I had two pet coons once," he told the boys who were spending the summer at Holiday Farm, "and I liked them. No hunter is going to trap these animals on my place if I can help it. I keep a watchdog that will scare them out of the cornfield. I built a henhouse they cannot enter. If the coons will keep out of my cornfield and the henhouse, they are welcome on the rest of the farm."

Cubby Lotor's accident did not prevent him from going to the next family picnic, though his paw was still sore. That was the night the Lotors started for the seashore.

The sea was only a few miles from Holiday Farm, but it took them a week or more to reach it. There were so many interesting things on the way that they did not hurry. As they followed the crooked stream, they had plenty of water in which to wash their food.

Early every morning they hunted for places where they might nap during the day. The weather was warm and they did not try to sleep together. Each found a crow's nest or a hollow in a tree or some such bed, or slept curled up in a crotch between two branches.

Every night they had a different sort of picnic. Once they found a bee-tree where wild bees had stored honey. They were very happy, for they liked honey. Cubby and his brothers and sisters had never tasted anything so sweet in their lives. Luckily for them, raccoon fur is so thick that bees cannot reach through it with their stings.

The corn picnic was one of the best ones. Father Lotor found the cornfield first, and he called. When the others heard his quavering signal, it did not take them long to join him. The juicy corn tasted so good that they could hardly wait to finish one ear before they began to husk another. They would have spoiled many ears in a short time if a dog had not heard them and chased them away from the cornfield.

One night they came to a large summer camp where some of the garbage pails were not covered. They helped themselves to pieces of sandwiches, cake and blueberry pie and cookies, and took them to the stream and washed them before eating them. The edge of the stream was muddy at that place, and the bits of cake and pie were rather queer by the time they had been squeezed and kneaded in the water. But the raccoons did not mind. They all seemed to wish to wash their food. Whatever happened to it while it was being washed pleased them well enough.

After they reached the seashore, they hunted clams when the tide was low. This was such fun that the Lotors dug and ate a great many.

They spent the autumn weeks wandering along the coast and up and down the neighboring streams. All this time their greatest pleasure was in hunting food and eating it. This was fortunate for them, for before cold weather comes raccoons should be fat—very fat indeed.

A raccoon should eat enough to grow very fat
before winter comes.

If they had lived in the South they could have found some food in the winter, but these raccoons were northerners and their hunting grounds would be covered with snow for many weeks.

They came to a little cave one night in November. Some boys who had played there the summer before had left a wooden box in one corner. The Lotors crept into the box. They did not bother to gather dry leaves for bedding. The bare boards were good enough. Their fur was so soft and thick they needed neither mattress nor blankets. It snowed the next day and the weather grew colder and colder. The Lotors did not even know it was cold. They were asleep.

During the winter there were times when the weather was not very cold. At such times the Lotors wakened and walked at night. They left their flat-footed tracks in the snow. But they found little to eat and they were drowsy, so they went back to their box and slept again.

CHAPTER IV

BLUE DAMSEL-FLIES

A PAIR of damsel-flies steered through the air toward some plants, called pipewort, that were growing in the shallow water at the edge of a quiet pool. They were flying low and they came rather gently and slowly, and not with the swift rush of their larger and stronger cousins, the dragon-flies, that were darting by in the air above them.

Mr. Damsel held Mrs. Damsel by a clasp at the tip of his tail that fitted, like a tiny bracelet, into a groove in her shoulders. That is a queer way of flying, but it is not the only odd thing these two little creatures did. In fact, there was not time, during the next half-hour, to stop wondering about one strange action before they were doing something else even more astonishing.

The color of Mrs. Damsel was soft grayish blue and black. Altogether she was only about an inch and a quarter in length, so there was not room for any part of her to be really large. Her head was much wider than it was long, and it reached from one round eye at the left side to another round eye at the right side. It was fastened to her thorax in such a narrow place that it looked as if it would drop off if she twisted it. But she never did lose her head, so the fastening must have been stronger than it seemed to be. She could eat and see with her head.

Her thorax was the second part of her body, and she used it in walking and climbing and flying. There were six jointed legs beneath and four thin, gauzy wings above.

The third part of her body was her abdomen. This was very slender, and much of the time she held it straight, though it was jointed and could be moved and bent. She could breathe with her abdomen, for, as perhaps you know, insects do not breathe through holes in their heads. She could do something else with this third part of her body too, as you shall see.

Mr. Damsel was somewhat the same size and shape as Mrs. Damsel but his color was brighter. Near his head and at his tail end he was glistening blue, as shiny as if he had been touched with some beautiful enamel paint.

They alighted on a pipewort stem. Mr. Damsel loosed the wee clasping bracelet at the tip of his tail and rested quietly on the little round blossom on the end of the stem. His four clear wings were folded close together along his slender body, and not held wide apart like the wings of a resting dragon-fly. His body stuck straight out in the air in a stiff position.

Mrs. Damsel turned and crept headfirst down the stem very quickly. Just as she reached the water she paused a moment and moved her wings. I am not sure

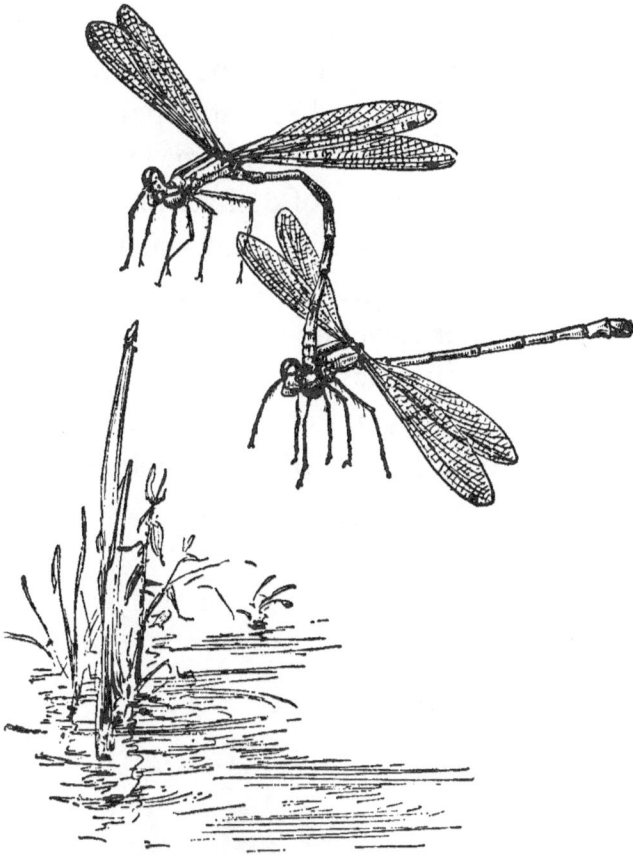

A pair of damsel-flies came through the air.

what she did with them, but they looked as if they were wrapped about her body in such a way that they made a little gauzy bag filled with air. Then she crept down the stem until she reached the bottom of the pond.

She did not seem at all afraid to leave the warm, sunny air and climb headlong into the cool water below. She went eagerly, as if she had a most important errand. And so she had, for Mrs. Damsel went into the pond to lay her eggs. Some kinds of damsel-flies push their eggs into stems and leaves of plants just under the surface of the water. Others have different interesting ways of putting their eggs into good places where they can hatch. But no kind has a better way than the blue damsel-flies of this story; these have the habit of always climbing down to the bottom of a pond before they find a suitable place for their eggs.

Mrs. Damsel went to the bottom of the pond to lay her eggs.

As soon as she reached the base of the pipewort stem, Mrs. Damsel walked slowly among the bits of soft, brown leafy rubbish at the bottom of the pond, and made her way carefully through tangles of little water plants. She poked the tip of her abdomen here and there, and left her eggs in places that were good nests for them. While she was busy in this way, she went nearly twenty inches from the pipewort stem down which she had climbed.

Now and then she thrust the slender third part of her body between her wings, which glistened in the water as if they held a bubble of air. I think she was breathing when she did this. There had been a time when Mrs. Damsel had lived day and night in the water for nearly a year. That was when she was young. At the tail end of her body she then had three flap-like gills with which she breathed. When she grew old enough to have wings and live in the air, she lost her gills, so she could not breathe that way any more.

Mrs. Damsel stayed under water a long time for a creature without gills. After she had been down for about a quarter of an hour, Mr. Damsel, who had been waiting on the plant overhead, flew away. But he did not go high into the air. He flew back and forth, a few inches above the surface of the water. As he flew he seemed to be watching for something. Now and again he alighted, and while he rested he still seemed to be watching.

He was not looking for food. Tiny midges and other insects he liked to eat flew near and he did not touch

33

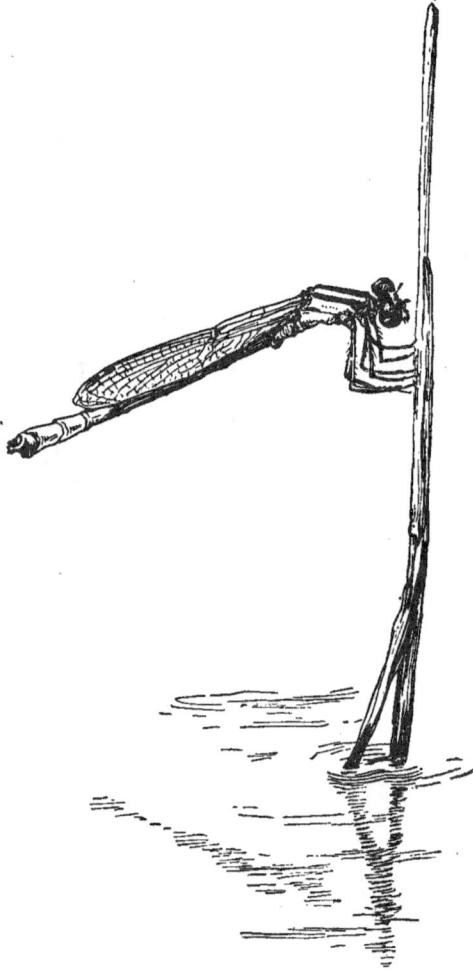

While Mr. Damsel waited he watched the surface of the water.

them. He was waiting for something that was more important than dinner, and he did not stop watching long enough even to snatch a mouthful.

Twenty minutes went by and Mrs. Damsel was still at the bottom of the pond laying eggs, and Mr. Damsel was still watching the surface of the water for something that had not come. Twenty-five minutes passed and Mrs. Damsel was still poking her abdomen among the stems of water plants as if she would never stop; and Mr. Damsel was flying back and forth just a few inches above the water with level flight—no higher, no lower, no faster, no slower.

Then suddenly something disturbed Mrs. Damsel. Perhaps the painted turtle that lived in the pond thrust her head too near. Mrs. Damsel did not walk twenty inches back to her pipewort stem to climb out of the water. She did not even wait to climb up the nearest stem of all. What she did was merely to let go of everything she was touching at the bottom of the pond and rise straight to the top—as straight as a bubble. While she was coming up through the water—her wings looked silvery, as if they still held a little air.

The instant Mrs. Damsel's head was above the water, Mr. Damsel saw her. He flew swiftly to her, and with a motion so quick that no one could see just how he did it, he clasped the little bracelet at the tip of his tail into the groove in her shoulders. Then, with hardly a pause, he continued his flight, pulling Mrs. Damsel out of the water as he went. As soon as her wings reached the air she shook them and spread them, and they seemed as fresh and straight and dry as if she had not been in the water at all.

As for the eggs at the bottom of the pond among the plants, neither Mr. nor Mrs. Damsel ever went back to see what became of them. Perhaps, if you live near a pond, you may like to go and see if they hatched. You can know a young damsel-fly, you may remember, by the three little flap-like gills on its tail.

A very young boy from Holiday Farm
liked to watch the damsel-flies.

CHAPTER V

VISITORS FROM THE SEA

THOUSANDS and thousands of little black sail-like objects were leaving the sea and heading into Holiday Stream. They looked like sails, tiny sails, moving on top of the sparkling water. But really they were fins on the backs of fishes. The alewives had begun their spring voyage.

The alewives belong to the Herring family. They are about twelve inches long when they are grown. Their backs are dark blue and their sides are silvery. That is the way they look when they are in the water.

The alewife belongs to the Herring family.

If you take one up in your hands and hold it in the sunshine for a moment, the flat overlapping scales look like glistening jewels. The scales on the back are deep blue, almost black, shading to paler blue. Those high on the sides are like opals, gleaming pink and blue and fiery gold and green. The lower scales are white, like pearls.

Most of the time the alewives live in the ocean, but in the spring they swim into fresh water.

The alewives waiting at the mouth of Holiday Stream were so close together that they touched one another. Their tails all pointed toward the sea, and their heads all pointed upstream. They were eager to go away from the ocean, and yet they waited. It was easy to see what held them back. The falls near the mouth of the stream were too high for them to climb. So they were trapped between the ocean to which they would not return and the falls they could not pass.

The tide was out. Shells and seaweeds which had been tossed by the last high water, now lay far up the shore in the sunshine. The barnacles clinging to the water-darkened piles of the nearest wharf showed how low the sea was, for it was only when the tide went out that the barnacles were uncovered.

Then something happened. The lowest barnacles that had been in sight were under water again. They had been clinging to the same spot all the time. They had not moved at all. As they had not gone down, the water must have come up. Yes, that was what had happened. The tide had turned. The sea was rising in the bay.

The waves slapped the smooth stones and swished along the shore. The nearest shells and seaweeds were no longer in the sunshine. They were in the sea again. As the water pushed farther and farther up the shore and crept higher and higher on the piles where the barnacles clung, it flowed into the mouth of Holiday Stream until it reached the falls.

The water that poured over the top of the falls was fresh. The water that washed against the foot of the falls was salt. And there, in the sparkling bay where the stream mixed with the sea, the little sail-shaped fins of the waiting fishes showed in the sunshine.

You can guess what was happening. The ocean was slowly climbing the falls and lifting the alewives with the tide. At last, where there had been high falls, there were hardly more than rapids.

The eager fishes waited no longer. They went up the rapids and struggled against the current with all their strength. Those hurrying in front were pushed by those that followed fast behind.

Many of the alewives mounted the rapids by plunging straight up the current. They went quick as flashes, their backs looking like blue streaks under the water. They did not leap out of the stream in climbing, as salmon and trout do, but took their chances in the current.

Some of the fishes were tossed back by the water, and they tried again and again to get through the rough places. Often they lost their balance in the swift and whirling current and were thrown over on their sides. Such fishes would flop along sidewise and push against the rocks with their fins.

It was hard work, but the fishes seemed to like

The water that poured over the top of the falls was fresh. The water that washed against the foot of the falls was salt. The ocean was slowly climbing the falls and lifting the fishes with the tide.

putting their strength against that of the stream. Not one of all the many thousands gave up trying. Not one left his struggling comrades and went back to swim easily in the sea.

They were very quick and they tried very hard, but there were so many thousands of them that they could not all crowd into the stream above the rapids before the tide turned.

As the tide went out and the rapids again became falls too steep for fish to climb, those that had not gone over the top halted. They waited with their heads toward the falls and their tails toward the sea. As the water went lower and lower and they sank with it, not one went back to swim in the broad ocean. They stayed crowded in the narrow mouth of the stream.

What held them there? They had spent most of their lives in the great salt sea. Why should they leave it and seek fresh water? How had it come about that the numerous fleet of tiny black sails had entered port together? What strange and wonderful feeling had come to them out in the ocean with power to turn them all so suddenly, all so eagerly, toward the gushing stream?

You might as well have asked the bobolinks why they had come. They were singing just then over the fields. There was joy in every note. What had happened to them in the pleasant South American places? Why did they fly back again every spring, gladly and with song?

The bobolinks had an errand in northern meadows, an errand of eggs and nests and young.

Well, the alewives had an errand too. I do not suppose they thought about it that way with their little brains. Perhaps there was something about the spring sunshine that drew them toward the shallow water near the shore. Perhaps some of the fresh water reached them as it rushed out of the mouth of the stream, and seemed good. Perhaps, in the springtime, swimming up into the fresh current seemed so pleasant that they could not help going.

We can only say "perhaps" because we do not really know how the fishes felt about their journey. But we may be sure that they liked it from the way they acted. And we may guess that if they could sing, they would have gone on their way with glad sounds, as the bobolinks go.

But after the alewives had pushed through the rapids at high tide, they were tired. Soon they came to a place sheltered by rocks, where the water was quiet as a pool. There they rested, swimming so slowly that they hardly seemed to move. It took them a week to reach Six-foot Falls, which was about half a mile away. The weather that spring was very cold, and the alewives were twice as long reaching the falls as they had been the year before, when the weather was warmer.

You might think Six-foot Falls too high for them to climb. They found a way at one side, however, where the rocks were like rough steps. They went up through that passage, and they went quickly. There was nothing slow about the alewives when they swam against swift water.

About a week after they left Six-foot Falls, the first of the alewives reached Holiday Pond, and the others

The fishes found a way to climb Six-foot Falls. They went up at one side where the rocks were like steps under the water.

At last the visitors from the sea found Holiday Pond.

followed when they were ready. They seemed contented in the pond and stayed there for some time. During their visit to Holiday Pond, the alewives laid their eggs.

As one alewife could lay sixty thousand eggs or more, there were soon a great many eggs in the pond. The eggs were small and sticky, and they were placed in gluey masses on stones and other objects rather near the shore.

After the alewives had laid their eggs, they did not seem to care much for the fresh water of pond and stream. Perhaps they were hungry, for they had not eaten since they left the sea. Be that as it may, they went out of the pond in small companies from time to time.

It was easy to tell when they were ready to go, for they gathered in little groups where Holiday Stream ran out of the pond. There they waited, their moving tails pointing downstream. Then, when they were ready, off they started, tail-first, for the ocean.

The eggs which had been left in shallow water were warmed by the sun, and they hatched in a few days.

When the little fishes began to swim, Holiday Pond was a lively place. The fresh water was good for their health, and they found plenty of food to make them grow. They hunted in the pond, and before the summer was over they looked much like their fathers and mothers, except for size.

They had grown to be two or three inches long, when they started on a strange journey. It was still warm weather and the pond quite as pleasant as ever, though perhaps there was less food in it. They may have been hungry, or tired of freshwater fare.

Nobody knows exactly why they left Holiday Pond, but leave it they did. They went down Holiday Stream, over Six-foot Falls, through the rapids, and into the sea. And they seemed to be having a good time all the way.

CHAPTER VI

THE PAINTED TURTLE

PICTA, the painted turtle, had made her nest, a dugout in the fine hot sand, on the shore of a lake with a name that makes a person smile to hear it. But to Picta a name did not matter. Lake Meddybemps, name or no name, had satisfied her for many years, and the sandy shore was what she needed for a nest. There the heat of the summer days could warm her buried eggs until at last her brood of babies, hatched by the sun, could creep their first journey to the lake.

Only one who knows how to tell the age of turtles could guess how many such nests Picta had dug on the shore of Meddybemps; and no one knows how many eggs she had laid in her life or how many of her son and daughter turtles had paddled out to hunt for polliwogs and other game. But this is certain: Picta will never meet the babies that hatched in the nest she dug on the shore of Lake Meddybemps that particular summer, for just after she had laid the last egg and covered the hole, who should come dancing along the shore but Eleanor!

Now Eleanor is one of those people who cannot

see a shy wild creature without wishing to become acquainted with it, and to meet Picta was a joy indeed. How Picta herself felt about the matter could be guessed from the way she struck out with her strong legs, struggling to push aside the hand that held her captive. Failing in this, she opened her mouth and hissed.

That hiss may have meant that Picta was afraid or angry; but it sounded so gentle, so almost like a sigh, that Eleanor smiled. "Don't hiss at me, poor, frightened Picta," she said, "for I will treat you so well that you will be quite comfortable and happy."

It did not seem that it would take much to satisfy Picta. Eleanor had heard of a pet turtle of one kind that ate bananas from the hand of his captor and drank water from a soup plate; and she did not know enough about the different sorts of turtles to understand that she could not make a painted turtle happy the same way.

So it happened that Picta was taken away from her sandy shore and given a ride in a rowboat. After trying many times, and always in vain, to climb the sides, she hid under the seat in the darkest corner. Later she was placed in a tub of water where she spent the night swimming, swimming, swimming, but getting nowhere at all. The next day she rode in a train and spent the minutes walking, walking, walking in a large tin can, but without finding any path that led out of her dark prison.

The journey over, new events awaited her. When she was hungry, she was offered a good ripe banana, but she tried to get away from it. When she was thirsty, she was

*Eleanor tried to make Picta happy
in a deep white pan.*

offered water in a soup plate, but she would have none of it. She just thumped, thumped, thumped around the edge of the room, poking her head against the wall as if hunting for a hole through which she could go.

Next she was put into a pretty white pan. When there was water enough, she swam around and around and around, but could never swim out of it.

When there was not much water in it, she stood on her hind feet and reached over the edge with her front feet and head and tried to pull herself out of it. But struggle and kick and stretch and push as best she could, she never reached far enough up to tumble over the edge and escape.

Picta reached over the edge of the pan with her front feet and tried to pull herself out of it.

One after another she was given the best comforts that Eleanor could find, but nothing really suited her. Even a giant box with four inches of fine sand in the bottom and a big pan of water sunk in one corner—even a turtle palace of that sort failed to make her happy. Some kinds of turtles might be pleased with things easy to provide, like a banana and a soup plate of water; but Picta was a painted turtle who for forty years, more or less, had been used to other things than those Eleanor could offer her.

Indeed, day after day passed by until six weeks had come and gone, and Picta was no nearer contentment than at first. She did not at all enjoy being a pet turtle.

There was only one thing she seemed to like, and that was hunting in the water for food when she was hungry. At first she would not eat when any one was near, but after a while she became used to company at mealtimes. She did not eat anything when she was out of the water; but if bits of fish or meat, either raw or cooked, were tossed into her pan, down would go her head and she would follow her funny little nose until she came very near one of the pieces. Then, no matter how still the food lay, Picta would be very careful to grab it into her mouth quickly and with a firm hold, as if it were trying to swim away from her.

If mealtime was the only comfort Picta had in all those weeks, it was natural that the only pleasure Eleanor found in her pet was in feeding it. It was fun to see the turtle push her head out of the water, looking and listening to be sure all was safe and quiet, and then poke it down to catch bits of food in the bottom of the water. If a piece was too big to swallow at a gulp, Picta had the most comical way of carving her meat. She would hold it firmly in her mouth and push it first with one front foot and then the other, one on each side, until it was torn smaller and smaller, becoming at last the right size to swallow easily. After one morsel had been eaten, Picta would put her head down and, like a dog following a scent, move slowly until she came to another bit. Then she would grab that in a hurry, and so with every fragment that she found, as if she expected her food to try to swim away.

When Eleanor held food in her hand under water, Picta would take it from her fingers in the same quick way; but the turtle would never reach up out of the water for her food.

Often Picta grabbed something in her mouth that she did not like. Then she would force it out quickly and push her front feet against the sides of her mouth as if she were trying to be rid of the taste. Then she would blow until little bubbles came up to the top of the water. That seemed to be her way of spitting out what she did not like. After such a time she seemed to sniff more carefully to avoid taking another bit of any bad-tasting stuff.

But a turtle is not a greedy creature, so the delight of eating could not keep Picta happy much of the time. For the most part, her brain seemed to hold one big idea, and that was freedom. She scraped around in the sand in her box hour after hour. She bumped her shell on the edge of her pan every time she crawled in and out. She went whackity thump and thumpity whack against the brick that made an island in her pan. In one way and another she knocked about in her efforts to escape, until she had battered and bruised her firm yellow under shell in four places. That was a pity, for it was a pretty under shell and until she had been taken prisoner there had not been a spot on its clear color. It began to look as if the shell that had lasted her forty years, more or less, would not stand the wear of forty weeks in her prison home.

By the first of September it was hard to know whether to be sorrier for Picta or for Eleanor. For Eleanor had promised to make her pet happy and she did not know how she could keep her promise. It is often easier to catch a wild creature than it is to put it into a place where it can be comfortable. Eleanor, by this time, was certain that nothing less than a big aquarium would do at all for a captive painted turtle, and this she could not provide. So she knew that she must set Picta free, but the question was, how and where?

She thought of sending Picta back to Meddybemps by express and asking the artist who spends his summers there drawing pictures about "when a feller needs a friend," to take the turtle back to her own place by the lake; for surely, if ever a turtle needed a friend, Picta did. But Eleanor did not know the artist well enough to ask such a favor. In fact she had not even met him when she visited at Meddybemps, so she thought she must take care of her own turtle.

She could not spare money enough to travel again to Meddybemps, but she looked at every other lake she saw when she was in country places, and at last she found one that she thought would satisfy a painted turtle in every way.

It was a little lake, so little that it was called a pond. At one side there were three sorts of flat circular leaves floating in the water. Some were those of the white water lily; some were those of the yellow pond lily, and some were those of a plant called the floating heart because of the shape of its leaves.

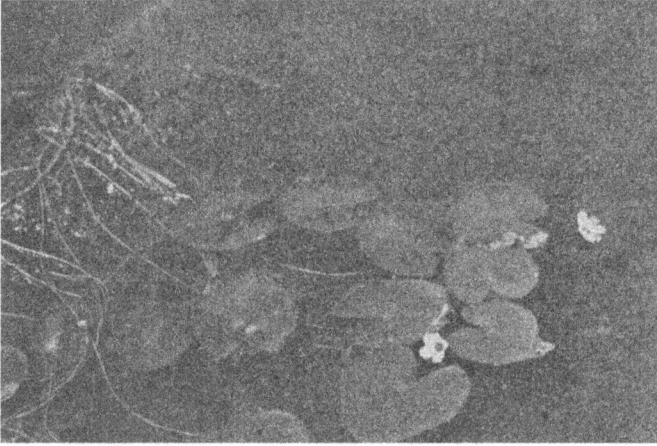

In the pond was a plant called floating heart because of the shape of its leaves.

Slender stems of pipewort plants with wee round heads grew both in the water and on the shore. But most of the pond was clear and without leaves, so clear that gravelly bottom could be seen far from the shore, and the reflections of the trees on the sloping banks were very beautiful.

Little spotted bronzy frogs were lazing about in the sun on the rocks far back from the water. Bigger green frogs were roosting on lily pads in the pond. Large, strong dragon-flies went overhead and back again, or settled to rest with all four wings spread wide apart. Slender blue and black damsel-flies were there, too, going low, very near the water, or resting on the pipewort with their wings folded close together.

Eleanor loved the pond because of all these things, but it was none of them that made her decide to bring Picta there; not frogs spotted or green, or dragon-flies or damsel-flies, or reflections in the water, or lily leaves or floating heart or pipewort. But while she was walking along one end of the pond, she saw a sunken log with just a bit of it up out of the water; and on that little wooden island a painted turtle was sunning itself. It was a little creature with a shell about four inches long, and not a full-sized one like Picta, whose shell measured six inches; but it was large enough to settle matters for

Eleanor loved the pond because of the white water lily that grew there.

55

Eleanor, for she thought that where one painted turtle lived in comfort another could.

So that was how it happened that Picta was given another train ride, this time only three hours long. She spent the night in a hotel, floating in a bowl of water, and breakfasted on bits of fried fish that she ate hungrily from Eleanor's hand.

Now was the day when Picta was taken to her little lake. When Eleanor reached the shore with her pet, she looked at Picta carefully so that she should never forget that a painted turtle has a smooth, nearly black upper shell, a clear yellow under shell, and gay splashes of red and yellow on its sides.

Eleanor put Picta down on the sandy shore some distance from the water and watched. The turtle stretched her head so far that the yellow on her head and the red on her neck showed, and she seemed to be looking and listening and smelling all at once. Then, very, very slowly, she walked to the water. Without haste, she slipped in and swam slowly about. Her restlessness was gone. She seemed in no hurry to go anywhere else. It began to seem as if Eleanor had kept her promise at last and that she had made her pet happy.

What happened next was a surprise to Eleanor; and as I do not understand the reason for it, I can only tell you just what took place and let you think what you like about it. The turtle had started off in a leisurely way toward the middle of the pond, putting her head up now and then to look about, when Eleanor called, "Good-by, little Picta," for she thought that was the last she should see of her pet. Picta just then turned and came back into the shallow water near the edge where Eleanor stood talking.

Picta swam back into the shallow water near the edge
of the pond where Eleanor stood.

Why did she come? Eleanor did not know nor do I. Did she just happen to come back when Eleanor called to her, or can it be that in her weeks of captivity Picta had learned to know Eleanor's voice and to think it was mealtime when Eleanor spoke? Did she come back to be fed? Be that as it may, the turtle made a dive and poked about near Eleanor as if hunting for food. Twice after that she started toward the middle of the pond and twice returned near the shore where Eleanor stood talking to her. Then away she paddled with a slow stroke, and when next she put up her head she was so far away that Eleanor could not see the head itself but only the ripples that circled around it in the water.

Eleanor walked along the shore till she came to the sunken log where she had seen the four-inch turtle sunning itself the day she had first visited the pond. There, on the same little wooden island, rested a turtle. It was not the four-inch one she had seen before. This one was only half as long. A moment later another just the same size as the one on the log swam near.

While Eleanor was laughing with delight about the pretty twin turtles, another and bigger turtle paddled slowly around the end of the log very near the shore, and put her head up and looked about. It was Picta!

At last Picta, the painted turtle, was free and happy.

Do you wish to know how Eleanor could be sure it was her pet? Well, Picta had a chipped shell, a three-cornered nick in the edge of her shell where she tucks her right hind foot. So Eleanor knew it was Picta come back again, and it pleased her to think that perhaps the turtle had come because of her voice. However that may be, Picta was hungry and began hunting for her food, and the tiny turtle on the log craned its neck to watch Picta while she hunted.

There Eleanor left them, and because her visit had been so pleasant she was glad that the place was named "Holiday Pond."

But to Picta a name does not matter. The little pond, name or no name, is suited to her needs. She has made no attempt to go out or away. She is content. And when another summer comes, the fine sand on the shore will lie warm in the sun and it may be hatching turtle eggs in a dugout nest.

CHAPTER VII

CARDINAL FLOWERS

THERE were some plants with gorgeous red blossoms growing at the edge of the brook that flowed out of Holiday Pond. They were too beautiful to disturb. Their straight stems, tipped with deep, rich red, were much lovelier beside the stream where the water reflected their color than they could have been if broken and placed in vases.

The people who lived at Holiday Farm never gathered these blossoms. They always left the cardinal flowers for the humming birds.

While the humming birds were waiting for these plants to blossom, they visited elsewhere. First, each spring, they found the rock columbines, the flowers of which, like groups of red horns lined with gold, held nectar that was good to sip. Before the columbines went to seed, the apple trees blossomed. For a few days the humming birds tasted the food served in dishes of pink and white apple petals.

Many insects came to the same banquet. Some of the smallest of these were doubtless eaten by the humming birds, for nectar was not the only food these birds enjoyed. They needed something besides sweet liquids to give them strength to fly far and fast, to build their nests, and to rear their young. They needed meat as well as drink, and they came to flowers for both nectar and tiny insects.

Bumblebees were often busy in the apple blossoms, and their big, fuzzy bodies seemed to be in the way of the humming birds, so the birds chased them off the tree. It was rather a funny sight to see the tiniest of birds darting after the largest of bees. They followed the black and yellow velvet-coated insects for ten or twelve feet, and then turned and flew swiftly to the fragrant blossoms as if in haste to enjoy the feast while there were no clumsy bumblebees about.

It was not until July that the cardinal flowers were ready. Meanwhile the humming birds spent eight or ten weeks visiting blossoms of various colors and many forms. They liked red best of all, however; and their slender bills were exactly the right shape to poke into flowers that held nectar in long tubes.

Neither in color nor in form were there blossoms more tempting than the cardinal flowers. So one July day, when these plants opened the earliest of their red buds, a humming bird came down to the water's edge.

At the time a boy and a girl were sitting on the bank near by. They were comradely cousins who were spending the summer at Holiday Farm; and they had been watching the young sandpipers wandering along the brook.

Suddenly something moved past them very near their heads. They heard several quick squeaks, fine squeaks, high-pitched and thin. At the same time there was a sound of tiny whirring wings. Then they saw a humming bird hovering before a cardinal flower. His back was glistening green. Underneath he was white and gray. The feathers of his throat were wonderful reds, seeming to change in the sunshine from ruby to scarlet or flaming orange. They gleamed like crimson jewels in the light.

The children on the bank looked at the ruby-throated humming bird among the cardinal flowers and at the colors reflected in the water below, and they thought that nothing else in the world could be so lovely.

After taking a sip from each open flower, the humming bird flew to a slender twig on a neighboring tree. There he rested for about ten minutes, preening his feathers and looking about. Then he made the rounds of the cardinal flowers again; and after taking a second rest on the same slender twig as before, he darted away to other flowery hunting grounds.

Each of the tall cardinal-flower plants had from ten to twenty red buds. These covered several inches of the upper part of the stem. The lowest buds were the first to open. Then those above blossomed. Last of all to flower were those at the very tip.

The most important parts of one of these flowers were the pistil and the stamens. The lower part of the pistil was a sort of seed pod, and attached to this was a slender part with a sticky tip, called a stigma. The

*The lowest buds of the Cardinal Flower
are the first to open.*

stamens were joined in such a way as to make a tube, and some dusty pollen grew on their tips. As the pistil grew longer, it pressed against the stamens and pushed the pollen out before its stigma became sticky enough to catch any of the pollen.

Now, unless some of the pollen grains fell on the sticky part of the pistil and from there found their way to the seeds, the seeds could never grow into plants. It takes pollen to make really live seeds. So if each cardinal flower lost its pollen before the pistil was ready for it, how could it ever have any seeds?

Indeed, there was only one way. Since each cardinal flower lost its own pollen, it must have pollen from another cardinal flower or else its seeds would perish.

Perhaps by now you have guessed what the humming birds did when they thrust their bills into the tube-shaped cardinal flowers for food? They brushed against loose pollen in newly opened blossoms, and carried it to the older blossoms with sticky stigmas. In this way they saved the lives of the seeds.

The humming birds, of course, did not know anything about the cardinal-flower seeds. But the feathers at the base of their bills grew in just the right place to catch the dusty pollen in one flower and to hit against the ready stigma in another.

The cousins from Holiday Farm came often to the border of the stream and the pond where the cardinal flowers grew, and if they waited quietly they were sure to see a humming bird. Often it would be a father humming bird with a ruby throat. Sometimes it would be a mother humming bird with a grayish white throat and a white tip on her tail. And before the topmost buds on the stalks opened, the young birds came down with whirring wings and squeaky voices.

Usually, though not always, only one bird came at a time. He had a thorough way of going into every open flower on a stalk and then choosing another stalk near by. He seldom skipped a flower unless something disturbed him. If he saw another humming bird coming too near, he would chase it away with a squeak of displeasure. He liked to be quite alone at mealtime.

Before the latest of the cardinal flowers lost their bright petals, the humming birds went on their long journey to Central America. There they found enough nectar in red, tube-shaped flowers and enough small, delicate insects to satisfy them until the next spring when the columbine was ready for them again in the north.

The cardinal flowers had their seeds to ripen before it was time for frost. The plants that were farthest away from the brook scattered their seeds in the mud, where they had a very good chance to grow. The plants that were in the stream began to drop their seeds into the water. Such seeds floated away. Some of them were washed ashore, where they sprouted and found root hold. But some of them drifted over Six-foot Falls and floated off to sea.

The cousins from Holiday Farm saw what was happening. They did not like to lose the seeds. They wished the humming birds to have a good garden another year. So they waded into the brook and picked all the seeds that had not floated away. These they planted in wet ground near the pond.

At last cold weather came. The tall stalks that had borne dark green, willow-shaped leaves and red flowers, were frozen. They became stiff and dry. Wind and snow broke the stems, which were no longer of use.

Near the roots of the old plants, however, were some shorter stems underground that did not become dry. They waited until the winter snows had melted. They waited until the high spring water had flowed over them and away. They waited until the summer sun was warm. Then they grew straight and tall, putting forth their long leaves, which were shaped much like those of willow trees.

When it was July again, their tips were gorgeous with blossoms. Near them were the younger plants that had been seeds the year before.

Before the earliest of the blossoms had been ready many hours, the humming birds visited them. It seemed as if the pollen-carriers had been waiting for the red buds to open.

CHAPTER VIII

NIM FAY, THE SAP-DRINKER

LITTLE NIM FAY had been drinking sap for forty-eight hours, and she did not seem to be thirsty for a while. She was only a few minutes more than two days old, and had taken a rather long drink for one so young. She had been standing all that time in one place on the stalk of a water plant, and she had been standing with her head down. She did that quite naturally, the first time she tried.

Nim Fay, of course, was an insect. No other kind of animal could have acted the way she did. The manners of insects, as you may have noticed, are apt to be queer.

Not being thirsty for the moment, Nim Fay pulled her beak out of the plant. There were three long bristles that she could push out from her mouth. She could suck juicy sap through her mouth parts somewhat as you can sip lemonade through a straw.

Perhaps the reason Nim Fay was not thirsty was that she could hold no more. Her skin was tight. Her plump little body was squeezed inside of it. She needed to molt.

This was the first time she had ever shed her skin.

Her mother and more than forty older sisters and a great many aunts and a great many more cousins were on the same plant at the time, but not one of them helped her. Her mother and aunts were drinking sap. So were her sisters and cousins, except those who were busy shedding their own skins.

However, the little two-day-old insect did very well by herself. She shrugged and wriggled until the tight covering ripped at the back like an old, thin dress. Inside of the stiff, torn covering was Nim Fay in a fresh, new, stretchy skin. All she needed to do now was to pull herself free. So she jerked her head out of the old mask, and she tugged her six legs out of their leggins. Then she walked to a place on the plant not far from her mother and sisters and other relatives, and rested.

Before long she was thirsty again. Molting had been rather tiring and she needed food. So she stood on the stalk with her head down and pressed the tip of her beak into the plant. This time she drank for about four days before she stopped to molt and rest.

When Nim Fay was twelve or fourteen days old, she had molted four times. She was now full-grown and was about one-twelfth of an inch long. She had no wings. In this she was unlike most full-grown insects. However, her mother and grandmother were both wingless, and so were all her relatives in the summer colony about her.

As she could not fly, Nim Fay stayed at home on her water plant. She drank sap minute after minute, hour after hour, and day after day. This was rather a dull sort of life, but she did not mind. She did not even seem

Nim Fay, the aphid, and her relatives,
lived on an arrowhead plant that grew in the pond.

to notice what went on in the air around her or in the water underneath.

Once the stalk of her plant was pulled under water by a frog that sat on the leaves. Nim Fay did not drown. Her little body was covered with waxy powder, and the water did not harm her. She had tiny wax pores in her skin, and the wax came through the pores and kept her body powdered.

When the frog jumped off the leaves, the stalk went up with a jerk that threw Nim Fay on the water. She did not sink. The wax on her body was a help to her. She could not really swim, but she walked across the water a little way. Then she came to the plant and walked up the stalk. She was not even wet.

Some of the rest of the colony were not so fortunate. While the stalk was under water, a little turtle swam near and swallowed a few of the insects. A fish saw some of them in the water and ate several, wax and all. A nearly grown tadpole helped himself to as many as he wanted. At the time, a bird with a forked tail was flying low over the water. He saw a plump, juicy insect moving, and caught it as he flew. Accidents like that are likely to happen to insects living near a pond.

Nim Fay's oldest daughter, Fay, fed herself sap when she was very tiny, just as her mother had done. Like her mother, also, she molted when she became too plump for her skin. But in one way she was different. She had four tiny wing-pads on her shoulders. Inside each wing-pad a wing was growing. The last time she molted, she pulled her wings out of the pads. They were rather wrinkled at first, but in a few minutes they were smooth and flat. They were dainty little wings, and thin and clear.

It was while Fay was standing on the tip of a leaf waiting until she was ready to fly that some people came down to the pond from Holiday Farm. There were several boys and girls who were spending the summer in the country, and an uncle who often came to see them.

The children had a new game that summer. They were trying to find a plant or an animal that their uncle did not know. So they pointed to a plant with broad leaves and lovely wax-white blossoms, and asked to be told its name. This, their uncle explained, was named "arrowhead" because its large leaves are shaped like the head of an arrow. Among its roots are tubers which are good to eat. Sometimes they grow to be as large as the eggs of hens. Indians, who used to gather such tubers late in the fall, liked to broil or roast them for a feast.

In the northwestern part of our country the Indian name for the plant was "wapatoo." Wapatoo Island and Wapatoo Valley were so named because the arrowhead grew in abundance in those places.

Cows like to eat the leaves, and often wade into the water for them. Fishes, called carp, devour the tubers so greedily that arrowhead plants soon disappear from places where there are any carp.

Like many other water plants, the arrowhead has two kinds of leaves. Those that grow under water are long and narrow. The plant breathes by means of these

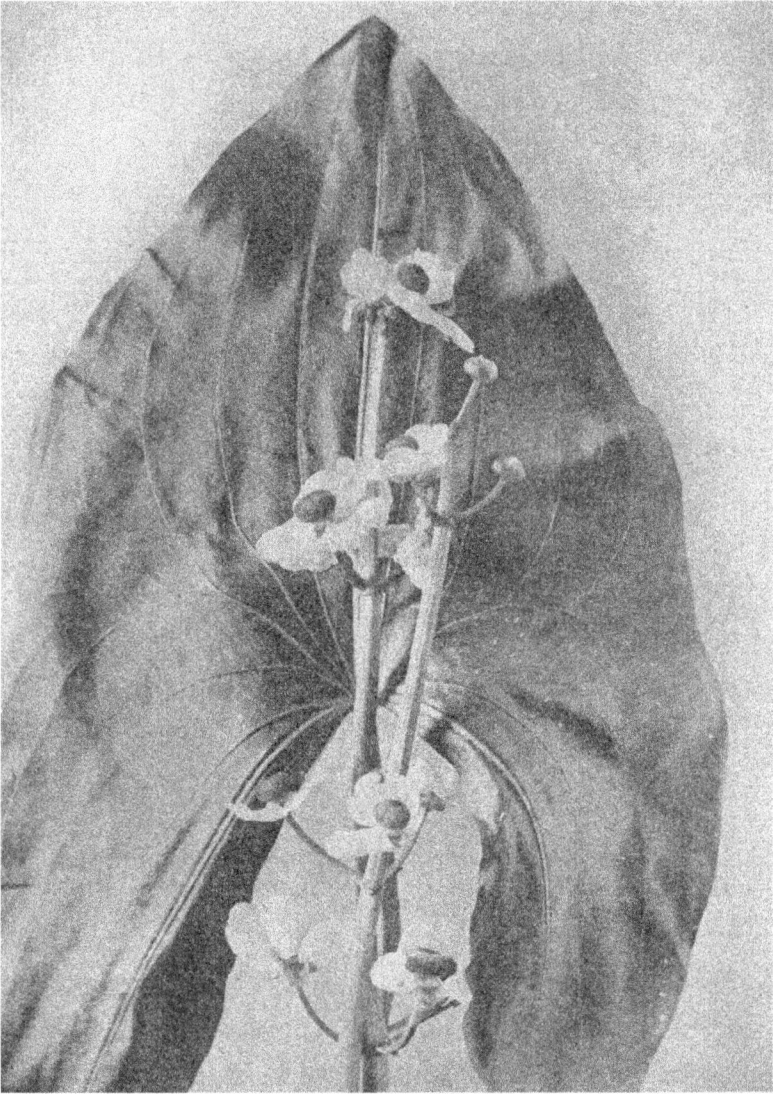

An arrowhead leaf and blossoms.

narrow leaves until it grows tall enough to push its broad, arrow-shaped ones above the water.

The arrowhead has also two kinds of blossoms, as the children from the farm saw for themselves. While their uncle was telling them about the plant, they waded into the water to look at it.

Just then one of the boys saw Fay at the tip of her leaf.

"Here, Uncle Ned," he called, "is something too tiny to have a name. Why, it is not much bigger than nothing at all! You don't know what *that* is, do you, now?"

The boy grinned. He thought it would be a good joke if he could find an insect so small that even his uncle did not know what it was.

Uncle Ned looked at the colony of small, reddish brown and greenish, wingless insects feeding on the stalk of the plant. Then he looked at little Fay. Her tiny wings were trembling. He liked a joke as well as the youngsters, so he, too, grinned.

"Well," he said, "about one hundred and seventy-five years ago a famous Swedish naturalist saw a colony of insects like that feeding on a water lily, and he called them *Aphis nymphaeae*, which is a Latin name. If you like an English name better, you may call your tiny insect a 'water-lily aphid.'"

At that very minute little Fay lifted her quivering wings and flew away.

"Where is it going?" the children asked.

Good-by to Arrowhead! Fay was ready to fly to a plum tree.

"To a plum tree at Holiday Farm," Uncle Ned told them.

"Then let's race and get there first," said one of the boys, and off they ran.

Of course little Fay, the water-lily aphid, did not know she was racing. But when she reached a plum tree, she stopped. She had not even noticed the oak trees or the elms or the maples or the pines. But there was something about a plum tree she could not resist. This seems rather strange, for she had never seen a plum tree before in her life. Neither had her mother. Neither had her grandmother.

They had spent all their lives on arrowheads.

But in the spring her great-grandmother, or perhaps it had been her great-great-grandmother, had grown up on a plum tree. She had drunk plum sap and thrived on it. When she molted the last time, she had thin, dainty wings. She was a spring migrant.

Now, as you know, migrants go on journeys. In the spring, swallows and humming birds and many other birds leave tropical countries and fly north. Alewives and shad and some other fishes swim out of the sea and into rivers and lakes. The migrant aphid on the plum tree had her spring journey, too. She flew to the pond and stopped on an arrowhead. A water lily would have done just as well, but she happened to find an arrowhead first.

Later in the season the swallows and humming birds fly south again. Alewives and shad swim back to sea. So perhaps it was natural for little Fay to stop when she came to a plum tree. Maybe the leaves smelled so good to her that she could not fly past them.

Nobody knows how Fay found her plum tree, but

In the spring aphids of this kind live in colonies on plum leaves.

find it she did. There is no doubt about that. It suited her exactly. She plunged her beak into the tender part of a twig and drank plum juice. She felt no need of anything different. Having grown up on a water plant, she was quite content to pass the rest of her life on a plum tree. So it happened that Fay never took another flight. She had used her wings to carry her from the pond to the orchard, and that was far enough.

Fay's large family of daughter aphids liked plum juice, too. They thrived on it and grew and molted, as young aphids should. They never had any wings, not even after they had shed their skins for the last time. As they were all satisfied with the plum tree, they did not need to fly.

All of Fay's daughters looked alike, and they all acted the same way. Little Apter was the oldest, so of course she molted first and became a full-grown aphid before her sisters did. She was about twenty days old when she molted the last time.

One day, while wingless Apter was waiting on the plum tree, an aphid with wings came to meet her. It was Alate, her mate, and he had flown all the way from the arrowhead in the pond to the plum tree.

Apter and Alate were rather busy for several days. It was getting late in the season, and their eggs must be made ready for winter. There was no nest to make, or anything of that sort, but Apter needed to find the right places to tuck her eggs.

On the branches of the tree, there were some small, scale-like buds that would not grow until the next spring. There were some tiny nooks and corners around these buds just the right size for aphid eggs. Of course Apter found one of these chinks for each of her eggs. She put one egg in a place and poked it in with a bit of sticky glue.

At first Apter's eggs were shiny green, but in a few days they became black as jet and stayed that way all winter.

Little Apter really did something very important when she glued her eggs to the plum twig. The nights were getting colder. Frosts would come. Leaves would fall. Sap would stop running in the plum tree. The ice would be deep on Holiday Pond. Arrowhead plants would be buried under snow. There would be no sap in all the frozen north for an aphid to drink.

But it did not matter. Apter's eggs were high and dry on the plum twig. The winter winds would blow, but they could not loosen the glue that held the eggs. The winter nights would be cold, but not cold enough to kill the tiny bits of life in Apter's eggs.

CHAPTER IX

SANDY THE SWALLOW

SANDY was taking his bath in Holiday Pond. He was only about five inches long but he liked a large bathtub. He was not sitting in shallow water and shaking himself, as a bathing robin does. He was taking a flying bath and splashing into the water here and there as he went. So it was pleasant to have plenty of room.

The water felt cool and comfortable as his hot little body dipped into it. He was glad, too, to stretch his wings in flight. Now and then he caught a nourishing insect as he flew. Bathing and flying and eating rested him when he was tired and hungry.

It was rather hard work digging a cave, and that was what Sandy had been doing. It was going to be a narrow cave about three feet long when it was finished. There was a great deal of dirt to dig out, and the only scraper he had was his bill and his bill was a small one. But Sandy did not mind hard work. He liked digging. The cave was such a nice one!

Browny thought so, too. Browny was Sandy's mate, and she liked the cave as well as he did. She liked it well enough to help dig it. So while Sandy was having his recess at the pond, she scraped busily with her little closed bill, and the cave in the sand bank grew deeper bit by bit.

The sand bank was one high side of a deep gravel pit near the pond. The man who lived at Holiday Farm left that side undisturbed. He called it the "swallows' wall," and said the birds were worth more to him than the dirt in the bank.

There was a swamp not far away with pools where mosquitoes bred, and the swallows took a great many of

The "Swallows' Wall" was one high side of a gravel pit near the pond. Here the birds lived in little dark caves.

their meals over there. They lunched, too, on tiny black hopping beetles that were flying toward the tomato plants in the garden or the potato field. And often they dined on some insects that would have done harm in the orchard if the birds had not eaten them.

The man of Holiday Farm was grateful for the help these swallows gave him, but he welcomed them for other reasons, too. It was pleasant to see them skimming and whirling through the air. They had no musical songs, but he liked to hear their chatter. When he was a boy he had lain for happy idle hours watching such birds busy at their caves, and he had never lost his friendly interest in them.

Before Browny had been working too long, Sandy flew back to the bank. There were about three hundred holes in the bank, for Sandy had many neighbors who had made their homes in caves. The holes looked very much alike, and Browny was nowhere in sight to tell him which one led into their cave.

Sandy did not lose his way, however. He found his own open door and, flying near it, he twittered a greeting to his mate. Chattering a welcome, Browny came out of the cave. The two birds talked for a moment. What they said no one but a swallow can know. They sounded as if they were giggling.

Then Browny flew away for her recess, and Sandy went to work. There was a swallow in almost every one of the three hundred neighboring caves, but each bird was too busy to talk with any one except his mate. So

There were many caves but Sandy did not lose his way.
He found his own home every time.

no one came to visit with Sandy, and he did a good bit of digging before Browny returned.

The caves in the sand bank were not all new ones. Some of them had been dug many years ago and had been in use every summer. The swallows that chose one of the old caves sometimes made it deeper, but usually there was not much to do by way of repairs except to make a fresh bed of straws and feathers at the inner end.

Although the door holes of the caves looked much alike, the caves themselves differed somewhat in shape and length. Some were only about two feet deep, and some were as much as four. Some were straight, and some turned around the corners of the stones in the bank. They all had the passageways gently sloping up from the holes. If any rain came in at the doors, the water fell and ran out again, and so the beds were kept dry.

Of course Sandy and Browny needed no straw and feather bed for themselves. But they made one, just the same, when their cave was long enough to suit them. And into that bed Browny put five pure white eggs.

The little eggs were kept warm. With a straw mattress and a feather bed under them and the downy breast of a parent bird tucked over them, there was no danger of their being chilled. Inside the white shells a wonderful growth took place. The yolks and whites of the eggs became bodies of young birds. Hour by hour, day and night, the tiny unhatched bodies grew and changed, until at last they were big and strong enough to break the shells that had held them safe and snug.

After the five baby swallows had cracked their eggshells, they cuddled close together in the nest. They wiggled and stretched and slept and, most of all, they ate.

That was a busy time for Sandy and Browny. They whirled and swept through the air. They hunted over the pond, over the meadow, over the swamp. They chased insects early and they chased them late. They brought food often to the young ones, who ate all that was given them and asked for more.

At first the young birds could not walk and Sandy and Browny brought the insects to the nest at the end of the cave. But by the time they were nearly the size of their father and mother, they came to the doorway to be fed. There was a narrow shelf of hard dirt just outside the hole. Sometimes the five youngsters sat there in a row to welcome Sandy when he came home from his hunt with his mouth full of tasty insects for them. When the parent bird left them, they hurried back into the cave out of sight.

One fine day there was a stir of excitement among the swallows. The young of Sandy and Browny were able to fly! So were the other young birds in the other caves! There were chattering and twittering and giggling sounds. The youngsters could fly, and all the swallows in the bank were going to celebrate. They were going to a picnic at Holiday Marsh.

The young birds started with fine courage, but they stopped to rest very soon. There was a telegraph wire a few rods from their bank. When they came to this,

The young swallows rested on the telegraph wire.

they perched on it in a row. It was just the right size to fit their little claws. They clung to it gladly. For a while it was more fun to balance there than to fly.

So the young birds rested on the telegraph wire in a row—hundreds and hundreds of them. Their parents urged them to fly away to the picnic at Holiday Marsh, but all they did was to flutter their wings and open their mouths. That was their way of teasing for food. They were begging their fathers and mothers to give them a picnic luncheon right there on the wire.

They were only babies after all. They had really done very well to fly as far as the wire. Perhaps the old birds were pleased that they had come even so far on the way. There was only one thing to do, and the patient old birds did it. They went hunting for insects. They flew over the pond or over the meadow or over the marsh, and came back with their mouths full.

How Sandy and Browny knew which of the hundreds of young birds belonged to their family, it would be hard to say. The children who were spending the summer at Holiday Farm had come to see the birds on the wire, and they thought all the young birds in the row looked alike. But Sandy and Browny seemed to know which of the fluttering, teasing wings belonged to their babies, and they put something into each of the five open mouths. The other parent birds were as patient and busy and careful as Sandy and Browny, and in time all the young birds were fed.

Food seemed to give the youngsters courage to fly again. So off they went with their fathers and mothers, who urged them and guided them. When they reached the marsh, they perched on the slender stems of the reeds and fluttered their wings and opened their mouths.

Of course Sandy and Browny knew what that meant. But they were really very cheerful and nice. They seemed happy to have their family with them. It was pleasant and sociable to be together, and, besides, they did not need to carry the food so far. It was much easier to feed the young Sandies and Brownies on the reeds of the marsh than to make a trip to the caves every time they caught a mouthful of insects.

The day passed gayly. The sun sank low in the west behind gray and rose-pink clouds. Evening came. Holiday Marsh grew dark. The stars gleamed high overhead. Above the distant tree tops the moon came into sight—full and round and golden.

Do you think the young Sandies and Brownies were back in their cave on a hot bed of dry grass and feathers? Not at all. They were roosting on slender reeds near old Sandy and Browny. They had moved. Their night home was now among the reeds and rushes, with the marsh beneath them and the open sky above them.

In the daytime they flew where they wished, and began to hunt insects for themselves. But they did not catch enough, and every time Sandy or Browny came near them, they sat on a reed or a twig and fluttered their wings and opened their mouths.

The bank swallows were not the only swallows camping at the marsh. There were the tree swallows that had nested in hollow trees in the woods or in bird boxes at the farm. They had dark, glistening, bluish green backs and pure white breasts. There, too, were the cliff or eave swallows that had come from their clay nests under the eaves of the farm barn. They were steel-blue and chestnut-red and brown and gray and white, and each had a whitish moon on its forehead. Besides these, there were the barn swallows that had left their nests on the beams and rafters of the open sheds at the farm. They had long, forked tails and chestnut-colored throats and steel-blue backs.

When the boys and girls from the farm came to the marsh, they had a game of telling which kind of swallows they saw. They always knew a bank swallow because it was mouse-colored above and white beneath and had a mousy brown band across its breast.

One afternoon while it was still warm, sunny weather, the children went to the marsh to play. But they did not play their swallow game. There were no swallows there. They waited until evening, but the birds did not come to roost among the reeds. The marsh seemed empty and lonesome. The swallows had left for another camp. This time Sandy and Browny and the young Sandies and Brownies and all the other bank swallows went on a long journey together. They flew by day and hunted insects as they went. They sometimes rested on telegraph wires along the way, and they passed many nights among the reeds in swampy places.

They flew through Mexico and Central America and into South America. Perhaps they camped in Brazil. Perhaps they went to Peru.

This much is certain: they stayed in southern countries while it was winter in the north.

When at last it was warm in North America again the bank swallows came back to their summer haunts. Some flew as far as Arctic places. Several hundred, however, stopped when they reached the caves near Holiday Pond. Among these were Sandy and Browny.

CHAPTER X

A POND-LILY'S GUESTS

ADVENA lives in Holiday Pond. She is a yellow pond-lily. Some people call her "spatter-dock," and some call her "cow lily." One day a man who studies plants said her name is "Advena." You may take your choice. Advena herself does not care what she is called.

The first time I visited Advena, I followed a path down a little hill to the pond. The path was narrow and led from side to side like the graceful trail of a snake. At the foot of the hill the path was bordered by sweetgale bushes, and I could not see the pond until I was very near it.

There were two large birds, with long necks and legs like stilts, standing by the quiet lake. They were herons. When they saw me come out from among the bushes at the end of the path, they were startled and flew away.

Next a family of sandpipers flew low across the water, speaking their alarm in sweet, quick tones.

Then the green frogs performed. They leaped from the shore to the pond, yelping wildly as they went. Their voices sounded somewhat like squealing pigs and somewhat like hurt birds screaming. But those funny frogs were in no pain. Jumping high into the air and splashing into the water with war whoops were their ways of scaring animals that came too near. They did not go quite together. They went one after another, quickly, like a package of exploding firecrackers. There seemed to be one hundred of the shrieking little jumping jacks.

A minute later all was quiet. There was not a frog to be seen or heard. A lot of circles, growing wider and wider, on top of the water, showed where the little yelpers had disappeared.

Sometime afterwards I saw one of the frogs again. He was sitting on one of Advena's big, flat leaves. His body was heavy enough to push the leaf down a little way so that all of him except his nose was covered with water. This time the frog did not jump or yelp. He was as silent and motionless as the leaf on which he sat. The back of his head and shoulders were almost as green as the leaf, and I was near enough to touch him before I saw him.

Often a frog visits Advena in this way. It is as if a neighbor came to rest on the porch and enjoy the view. Sometimes he helps himself to a bit of lunch if he sees anything that he likes to eat. He is so quiet while he waits that flying insects alight near him and water insects swim close to the leaf.

A colony of tiny insects, called aphids, spend the summer with Advena. They camp on the upper side of a long, trailing leaf-stem if one happens to lie on top of the water. Another favorite camping place is the under side of a leaf when Advena grows tall enough to push her leaves into the air. They are the same kind of little sap-drinkers as Nim Fay, who lived on the arrowhead. So of course the winged ones fly to the plum trees when they are ready to leave their summer camp.

Don and Acia visit Advena every summer. They are dark-colored beetles with rather narrow bodies that glisten in the sunshine. On almost any summer day they may be seen resting on Advena's leaves, although they are quick to fly if any one comes near.

Advena, the yellow pond-lily.

Don and Acia visit the yellow pond-lily every summer.
They are quick to fly if any one comes near.

Don does not do much except to rest and fly and eat. He does not have a busy summer. But Acia finds a good place for her eggs.

The place she chooses is the under side of one of Advena's leaves, but it must be a leaf that lies flat on top of the water. Acia glues her eggs on the wet under side of the leaf, but she does not go into the water to do so. She stands on top of the leaf and bites a hole in it. Then she pokes the tip of her body through the hole and places her eggs in a circle around the hole. She covers them with a substance that looks like gelatine.

The tiny white eggs stay in their nest of glue for about a week and a half before the young Dons and Acias hatch. The young ones do not find anything that satisfies them on Advena's leaf, so they go on a journey. They travel as far as the underground stem of the yellow pond-lily, the part that grows in the oozy bottom of the pond.

They look nothing whatever like their father and mother. They are little white grubs down in the soft black mud. They need food to eat and air to breathe, and where do you suppose they find it?

There is plenty of air in Advena's stems. She breathes with her leaves, and her stems have little cells filled with air. If her stems are broken under the water, bubbles of air come up to the top of the pond.

The little white grubs have sharp spines at the tips of their tails. With these spines they bore into the stem of the pond-lily and break some of the air-cells. When the air comes out of the stem, the little grubs take it into their breathing pores. In this way they can breathe while in the water even though they have no gills.

They find food, too, in the yellow pond-lily. They nibble round holes in the underground stems and eat all they need to make them grow.

After they are as large and plump as Don and Acia grubs ever grow to be, each one spins a silken cocoon. The silk comes from glands that open in the mouth, and with it the grub makes a cocoon that is tough and brown. This strong case is water-tight and air-tight. The water cannot soak into it, and the air cannot get out.

In such snug sleeping bags among Advena's roots, the young insects rest until they have changed from white water grubs to beetles with wings. Then they nibble holes in the cocoons and creep out into the water.

But they do not stay there long. Their water days are over. They rise to the top of the pond and climb up Advena's blossom stalk or other handy ladder.

At last they look like their father and mother, all dark and shiny in the sunshine. When you come too near, away they go on wings as quick as were those of old Don and Acia.

To watch one of Advena's leaves on a quiet, sunny summer day is like looking at a moving picture. A slender damsel-fly, with wings held lengthwise along its body, rests lightly on the big, flat, heart-shaped leaf for a while. A long-legged water strider comes skimming and skipping over the surface of the water and takes several hops across the broad leaf. A lot of shiny whirligig-beetles dart around in quick circles in the water near by. A young frog rests its chin on the rim and looks and waits for some time before it swims away.

If you choose to watch an old yellow leaf, sunken a little so that one edge is covered with water, you are likely to see some tiny fishes poking against it and swimming across it.

A snail may come, too—a water snail with the coils of its shell so flat that both sides look almost alike. This snail comes to the surface to change the air in its air-sac. The used air comes bubbling out, and then the sac fills with fresh air. The snail can hold this air in the sac and use it while under water. Perhaps, during its visit to Advena, the snail may scrape off and eat a bit of the ripe and mellow leaf.

Many of Advena's guests do nothing whatever in

Snails that live in the water often visit the plants in the pond.

return for the food and comfort they enjoy while visiting her. Others, however, help her very much. Indeed, the lives of her seeds depend on the visits of certain of her guests. Among these are bees and flies that come to her blossoms.

The outside green sepals that protect the bud of a yellow pond-lily do not stay green as the sepals of a rose do. They turn bright yellow and form the showy part of the flower. Inside of them are short, scale-like petals and rows and rows of short, flat, flap-like stamens. The petals and stamens are in a circle around the base of the big greenish box full of young seeds. The seeds cannot live and grow unless some pollen is sprinkled on the sticky top of the seed-box.

There is plenty of pollen on the stamens, but it does not ripen in time to do any good to the seeds in the same flower. So that is how the small bees help Advena. They go into yellow pond-lily blossoms that are old

95

enough to have ripe pollen. They gather as much as they can. They need it for "bee bread" for their young bees to eat. While they are busy inside the flower, their bodies become dusty with pollen. Next they fly to a younger blossom which is open only a little way. They walk over the sticky top of the seed-box, and some of the yellow dust stays there, where Advena needs it for her seeds. After that they creep among the short petals and help themselves to a little sweet nectar they find there. They like to taste some of it, and some they carry away. They need nectar to mix with pollen when they make their "bee bread."

Certain large flower flies come to pond-lily blossoms to sip nectar and eat pollen, and they carry the golden, live dust from the older flowers to the younger ones as the bees do. They are the syrphus flies, and some of them are as large as the little bees that they meet in Advena's blossoms.

The bees and the syrphus flies never know that they help the plants they visit. They do not know when pollen shakes off their bodies and falls on the sticky tops of the seed-boxes in the blossoms. Advena herself does not know that the lives of her seeds depend on such flower insects.

People, however, can watch Advena and see how her guests behave. And is it not rather comforting to know that some of her visitors treat her well? So well, indeed, that yellow pond-lilies are abundant, and "spatter-docks" hold their golden globes above the quiet water in many places.

CHAPTER XI

THE DUSKY DUCKS

THE latest of the yellow pond-lilies had gone to seed. Rana, the frog, had stopped hunting for the season. Most of the pond was frozen over. The only open place was near the bubbling spring.

In spite of the cold, however, guests still came to Holiday Pond. The dusky ducks paddled happily about near the spring. They drank some of the icy water without a shiver. They poked their heads under the edge of the ice and pulled up some chilly stems of arrowhead for an early breakfast, and it tasted good to them. Then they flew to the sea, where they swam and hunted until they were thirsty again for fresh spring water.

It was not only in winter that the dusky ducks came to Holiday Pond. They were there at other seasons, too. Indeed, two of them, old Drake and Duck Anas, had begun to stop there for meals in April.

That was after they had been badly frightened at Reedy Lake, a few miles away. They had been visiting that large lake during March and early April; but one morning about sunrise they heard a sudden frightening

The dusky duck poked his head under the edge of the ice and pulled up some chilly stems for breakfast.

noise. At the same moment they caught sight of an unpleasant man with a gun.

They flew up swiftly, almost as if they had jumped quite high into the air. Both Drake and Duck Anas said "Quack" several times rather quickly and in scared tones. As they flew they showed the silvery white linings of their wings.

After they had gone several miles, they looked down and saw Holiday Pond. The water was still and peaceful in the early morning. Nothing seemed to be stirring except a small flock of ducks that had come down from Holiday Farm for a breakfast swim. The farm ducks were so contented and unafraid that Drake and Duck Anas stopped near them for company.

The dusky ducks did not look like the farm ducks. They were dark brown, with streaky buff-colored heads and necks. Their wings each had a black-bordered patch of beautiful violet-blue feathers near one edge.

Although the dusky ducks came often to Holiday Pond after that, the people at the farm seldom saw them. These ducks were timid and visited the pond only when it was quiet. Early in the morning before dawn, evenings, and moonlight nights were the times they chose.

Late in April, Duck Anas hid herself in a brushy corner of Holiday Pasture. The pasture was next to the woods, and some old trees had fallen across one corner during a heavy windstorm. Their trunks made a sort of fence, past which the cows could not crowd. Some bushes had grown in a thick mass around a stump. On one side of the stump was a sheltered little hollow. It was in this hollow that Duck Anas chose to hide.

She stayed there almost a month. When she was very hungry, she crept to a place where some tender, juicy weeds were growing. Sometimes she was thirsty, and then she would go quietly to the little brook in a bog not far away.

Old Drake knew where she was, but he was careful to keep her secret, and not even Lotor, the coon, saw him when he went to visit Duck Anas.

The hollow where the dusky duck sat night and day for four weeks was lined with dry grass and leaves. There was a soft, warm layer of downy feathers, too, and on the down were ten eggs. The eggs were almost cream-colored, with just a tinge of pale green.

The ducklings inside the shells kept their mother waiting about twenty-eight days before they were hatched. But after they had broken their shells and dried their first, fluffy down, they did not keep her many hours at the nest. They were ready to go with her when she spoke softly to them and started for a walk.

Like their mother, the young ducks all had a queer way of walking. They were boat-shaped, and their legs were back under their bodies not far from their tails. Their three front toes were connected with flaps or webs of skin, so that their feet were rather like paddles.

Their bodies were, indeed, better shaped for swimming than for walking, and it is not surprising that Duck Anas led them to water. When they came to the first pool in the bog, they went into it and began to swim. They did not need to be taught how. For some time they lived contentedly in the pools and the brook. When they were frightened, they hid among the clumps of grass and sedges.

There were so many wrigglers, or young mosquitoes, in the bog pools that the man who owned Holiday Farm thought that he might need to drain the bog to get rid of them. But the dusky ducks liked to eat wrigglers, and they feasted on thousands and thousands of them, so that there were not so many mosquitoes as usual that spring. Those wrigglers that did escape the ducks and become mosquitoes flew into the air, where the swallows were waiting for them. So the bog did not need to be drained at all.

Wrigglers were not the only meat the ducklings ate. Many kinds of water insects were caught in their flat, broad bills. Flies that came down to the water plants were quickly grabbed and swallowed. Aphids that crowded thickly on arrowhead and pond-lily stems made many a luncheon for the ducks. That was one reason why there were not more aphids to fly to the plum trees in the fall. So it was that the wild ducks helped take care of the fruit in the orchard.

Sometimes Duck and Drake Anas led their young ones away from the brook to jolly moonlight picnics on land. At such times they lunched on grasshoppers and crickets and beetles. Now and then they ate cutworms.

The dusky ducks liked green salads, and they gathered them fresh. One minute a tender, juicy plant would be growing beside the brook, and the next minute it would be slipping out of sight in a duck's bill.

When the plants were old enough to have seeds, the ducks feasted on those. As twenty thousand seeds make only a fair-sized meal for a duck, you can guess what became of a lot of the seeds of smartweeds and sedges that summer.

You may think, too, that it was very fortunate for Drake and Duck Anas that they did not need to gather food for the ducklings. It would have been a hard summer for the old ducks if those ten greedy young ones could not have gathered their own food.

The ducklings needed care in other ways, however. Their father and mother led them into the safest places they knew, and they taught them to be more and more timid.

One day in the spring, while they were still very young, they heard shouts near them in the bog. Two boys from Holiday Farm were hunting for pitcher-plants. Duck Anas said "Quack" to the young ones in a tone that meant "Hide." Then she went away and left her babies.

But she did not go high into the air and fly quickly, as she did that day when the man at Reedy Lake tried to shoot her. She flew slowly, in a tumbly way, as if she had a broken wing. She fluttered very close to the ground.

"Look," said one of the boys, "there's a wild duck, and it has been hurt. Let's catch it and see if Uncle can mend its wing." So the boys tried to catch Duck Anas.

They ran until they were out of breath, and the mother duck kept just a little ahead of them all the time. Then, after they had gone a long way, Duck Anas lifted her strong wings and flew rapidly out of sight.

Then the boys laughed. They had seen other birds do that same trick. They said: "She fooled us all right. She led us away from that place in the bog. She must be a mother duck. Probably there is a brood of young ones in the brook. Let's go back and find them."

They hunted and hunted, but they did not catch a glimpse of a duckling. Each little bird had obeyed the mother's "Quack" and had hidden among the clumps of sedges.

After the boys had given up the search and gone home, Duck Anas slipped quietly into the water. She said "Quack" softly and in a tone that meant "Come." One by one the little ducks left their sedges and gathered around their mother. They had a glad, safe feeling. The boys from the farm would have done them no harm, but they did not know that. All dusky ducks must grow to be very, very timid, and they were learning how.

Although the young ones could walk and swim even while they were in their first suits of down, they could not fly until their wings had grown large and strong. By August, however, they no longer needed to be left behind, hiding among the sedges, when Drake and Duck Anas went for long flights. They could go too.

One day in September the whole Anas family flew together to Holiday Cove. After the young ducks had

had their first swim in the sea, they felt hungry. So they had a shore-dinner.

There were snails in little pools left when the tide went out. And there were blue mussels, too, among the pebbles. It was fun for the ducks to break the shells that covered such food. They did not need any nutcrackers to help them. Their flat bills were strong enough. For a salad they ate plenty of eelgrass.

As the weather grew colder in the fall, the Anas family spent more and more time at the cove and on the sea. They often met other dusky ducks swimming over and between the ocean waves. Sometimes they joined large flocks of them.

Whenever the ducks were thirsty, they sought fresh water. Sea water was too salty for them to drink. For a while they visited the streams at night, when no people were near. But in time the streams were frozen over. Then Drake and Duck Anas remembered the bubbling spring at Holiday Pond. They had been there to drink the winter before. So they led the way, and others of the flock followed.

One bitterly cold night when the ducks visited the pond, they found that the ice had crept to all sides of the spring and nearly covered it. The pond lay still under a thick blanket of new snow. There was only a little spot where there was open water, and the ducks crowded and pushed each other to reach it. The ice at the edge was thin and broke under their weight. They drank and drank. Would even this little spot be frozen over next time they came?

Holiday Pond lay under a thick blanket of snow.

The next day the man of Holiday Farm happened to pass the pond. He saw the tracks of the ducks. He noticed how their webbed feet had packed the snow on the ice about the spring. He looked at the smoke curling up from his own comfortable home. He felt safe, with shelter and warmth and food and water. Then he looked again at the tracks on the pond. Little points of ice were reaching into the few inches of clear water about the spring. The wind was blowing from the north.

The man turned suddenly away from the pond. He went to his woodshed and came back with an ax and a shovel. He shoveled the snow away from all sides of the spring. He broke the ice back for several feet and pushed it out of the way on the shore.

That evening he came and stood by some cedar trees near the pond. Soon he heard a sound of wings in the air and then a splash of water at the spring. He

105

smiled and went quietly back to his fireside. He could enjoy the comforts of his home better because the dusky ducks were quenching their thirst.

www.ingramcontent.com/pod-product-compliance
Lightning Source LLC
Chambersburg PA
CBHW032017090426
42741CB00006B/631